The Poetry Of Francis Thompson
Volume 1

Francis Thompson was born in Preston on Lancashire in December 18th, 1859.

Educated at Ushaw College, near Durham he studied medicine at Owens College in Manchester. However the medical profession held little interest to him but writing did. He moved to London in 1885 but found no success and was quickly reduced to selling matches and newspapers for a living.

Ill health offered up opium as a solution and to this he quickly became addicted. Life became increasingly difficult and soon Francis was no more than a vagrant living on the streets, chiefly around Charing Cross and along the Thames. In 1888 he sent some poems to the publishers of the Merrie England magazine who were Wilfrid Meynell and his noted poet wife Alice. They quickly sought him out, arranged for his housing and other necessities as well as medical treatment and encouraged him to write more. This culminated in the publication of his book 'Poems' in 1893.

The book, including the seminal 'Hound Of Heaven' was recognised as a great work by many critics at the time and encouraged further volumes; Sister Songs in 1895 and New Poems in 1897. Years of ill health, addiction and vagrancy had taken their toll upon Francis and he moved to Storrington in Wales where we continued to write though by now he was invalided. An attempt at suicide was aborted by a vision he had of Thomas Chatterton, the teenage poet, who had committed suicide a century earlier.

However his remaining years were few in number and he succumbed to tuberculosis at the age of 48 on November 13th, 1907. He is buried in the Catholic section of Kensal Green Cemetery in London.

G.K. Chersterton said "with Francis Thompson we lost the greatest poetic energy since Browning."

Index Of Poems

I0836454

Gilded Gold
Dream Tryst

The Hound Of Heaven

I fled Him down the nights and down the days
I fled Him down the arches of the years
I fled Him down the labyrinthine ways
Of my own mind, and in the midst of tears
I hid from him, and under running laughter.
Up vistaed hopes I sped and shot precipitated
Adown titanic glooms of chasme d hears
From those strong feet that followed, followed after
But with unhurrying chase and unperturbe d pace,
Deliberate speed, majestic instancy,
They beat, and a Voice beat,
More instant than the feet:
All things betray thee who betrayest me.

I pleaded, outlaw wise by many a hearted casement,
curtained red, trellised with inter-twining charities,
For though I knew His love who followe d,
Yet was I sore adread, lest having Him,
I should have nought beside.
But if one little casement parted wide,
The gust of his approach would clash it to.
Fear wist not to evade as Love wist to pursue.
Across the margent of the world I fled,
And troubled the gold gateways of the stars,
Smiting for shelter on their clange d bars,
Fretted to dulcet jars and silvern chatter
The pale ports of the moon.

I said to Dawn - be sudden, to Eve - be soon,
With thy young skiey blossoms heap me over
From this tremendous Lover.
Float thy vague veil about me lest He see.
I tempted all His servitors but to find
My own betrayal in their constancy,
In faith to Him, their fickleness to me,
Their traitorous trueness and their loyal deceit.
To all swift things for swiftness did I sue,
Clung to the whistling mane of every wind,
But whether they swept, smoothly fleet,
The long savannahs of the blue,
Or whether, thunder-driven,
They clanged His chariot thwart a heaven,
Plashy with flying lightnings round the spurn of their feet,
Fear wist not to evade as Love wist to pursue.
Still with unhurrying chase and unperturbed pace

Deliberate speed, majestic instancy,
Came on the following feet, and a Voice above their beat:
Nought shelters thee who wilt not shelter Me.

I sought no more that after which I strayed
In face of Man or Maid.
But still within the little childrens' eyes
Seems something, something that replies,
They at least are for me, surely for me.
But just as their young eyes grew sudden fair,
With dawning answers there,
Their angel plucked them from me by the hair.
Come then, ye other children, Nature's
Share with me, said I, your delicate fellowship.
Let me greet you lip to lip,
Let me twine with you caresses,
Wantoning with our Lady Mother's vagrant tresses,
Banqueting with her in her wind walled palace,
Underneath her azured dai:s,
Quaffing, as your taintless way is,
From a chalice, lucent weeping out of the dayspring.

So it was done.
I in their delicate fellowship was one.
Drew the bolt of Nature's secrecies,
I knew all the swift importings on the wilful face of skies,
I knew how the clouds arise,
Spume d of the wild sea-snortings.
All that's born or dies,
Rose and drooped with,
Made them shapers of mine own moods, or wailful, or Divine.
With them joyed and was bereaven.
I was heavy with the Even,
when she lit her glimmering tapers round the day's dead sanctities.
I laughed in the morning's eyes.
I triumphed and I saddened with all weather,
Heaven and I wept together,
and its sweet tears were salt with mortal mine.
Against the red throb of its sunset heart,
I laid my own to beat
And share commingling heat.

But not by that, by that was eased my human smart.
In vain my tears were wet on Heaven's grey cheek.
For ah! we know what each other says, these things and I; In sound I speak,
Their sound is but their stir, they speak by silences.
Nature, poor step-dame, cannot slake my drouth.
Let her, if she would owe me
Drop yon blue-bosomed veil of sky
And show me the breasts o' her tenderness.
Never did any milk of hers once bless my thirsting mouth.

Nigh and nigh draws the chase, with unperturbe d pace
Deliberate speed, majestic instancy,
And past those noise d feet, a Voice comes yet more fleet:
Lo, nought contentst thee who content'st nought Me.

Naked, I wait thy Love's uplifted stroke. My harness, piece by piece,
thou'st hewn from me
And smitten me to my knee,
I am defenceless, utterly.
I slept methinks, and awoke.
And slowly gazing, find me stripped in sleep.
In the rash lustihead of my young powers,
I shook the pillaring hours, and pulled my life upon me.
Grimed with smears,
I stand amidst the dust o' the mounded years
My mangled youth lies dead beneath the heap.
My days have crackled and gone up in smoke,
Have puffed and burst like sunstarts on a stream.
Yeah, faileth now even dream the dreamer and the lute, the lutanist.
Even the linked fantasies in whose blossomy twist,
I swung the Earth, a trinket at my wrist,
Have yielded, cords of all too weak account,
For Earth, with heavy grief so overplussed.
Ah! is thy Love indeed a weed, albeit an Amaranthine weed,
Suffering no flowers except its own to mount?
Ah! must, Designer Infinite,
Ah! must thou char the wood 'ere thou canst limn with it?
My freshness spent its wavering shower i' the dust.
And now my heart is as a broken fount,
Wherein tear-drippings stagnate, spilt down ever
From the dank thoughts that shiver upon the sighful branches of my mind.

Such is. What is to be?
The pulp so bitter, how shall taste the rind?
I dimly guess what Time in mists confounds,
Yet ever and anon, a trumpet sounds
From the hid battlements of Eternity.
Those shaken mists a space unsettle,
Then round the half-glimpse d turrets, slowly wash again.
But not 'ere Him who summoneth
I first have seen, enwound
With glooming robes purpureal; Cypress crowned.
His name I know, and what his trumpet saith.
Whether Man's Heart or Life it be that yield thee harvest,
Must thy harvest fields be dunged with rotten death ?

Now of that long pursuit,
Comes at hand the bruit.
That Voice is round me like a bursting Sea:
And is thy Earth so marred,
Shattered in shard on shard?

Lo, all things fly thee, for thou fliest me.
Strange, piteous, futile thing;
Wherefore should any set thee love apart?
Seeing none but I makes much of Naught (He said).
And human love needs human meriting
How hast thou merited,
Of all Man's clotted clay, the dingiest clot.
Alack! Thou knowest not
How little worthy of any love thou art.
Whom wilt thou find to love ignoble thee,
Save me, save only me?
All which I took from thee, I did'st but take,
Not for thy harms,
But just that thou might'st seek it in my arms.
All which thy childs mistake fancies as lost,
I have stored for thee at Home.
Rise, clasp my hand, and come.
Halts by me that Footfall.
Is my gloom, after all,
Shade of His hand, outstretched caressingly?
Ah, Fondest, Blindest, Weakest,
I am He whom thou seekest.
Thou dravest Love from thee who dravest Me.

To A Poet Breaking Silence

Too wearily had we and song
Been left to look and left to long,
Yea, song and we to long and look,
Since thine acquainted feet forsook
The mountain where the Muses hymn
For Sinai and the Seraphim.
Now in both the mountains' shine
Dress thy countenance, twice divine!
From Moses and the Muses draw
The Tables of thy double Law!
His rod-born fount and Castaly
Let the one rock bring forth for thee,
Renewing so from either spring
The songs which both thy countries sing:
Or we shall fear lest, heavened thus long,
Thou should'st forget thy native song,
And mar thy mortal melodies
With broken stammer of the skies.

Ah! let the sweet birds of the Lord
With earth's waters make accord;
Teach how the crucifix may be
Carven from the laurel-tree,
Fruit of the Hesperides
Burnish take on Eden-trees,

The Muses' sacred grove be wet
With the red dew of Olivet,
And Sappho lay her burning brows
In white Cecilia's lap of snows!

Thy childhood must have felt the stings
Of too divine o'ershadowings;
Its odorous heart have been a blossom
That in darkness did unbosom,
Those fire-flies of God to invite,
Burning spirits, which by night
Bear upon their laden wing
To such hearts impregnating.
For flowers that night-wings fertilize
Mock down the stars' unsteady eyes,
And with a happy, sleepless glance
Gaze the moon out of countenance.
I think thy girlhood's watchers must
Have took thy folded songs on trust,
And felt them, as one feels the stir
Of still lightnings in the hair,
When conscious hush expects the cloud
To speak the golden secret loud
Which tacit air is privy to;
Flasked in the grape the wine they knew,
Ere thy poet-mouth was able
For its first young starry babble.
Keep'st thou not yet that subtle grace?
Yea, in this silent interspace,
God sets His poems in thy face!

The loom which mortal verse affords,
Out of weak and mortal words,
Wovest thou thy singing-weed in,
To a rune of thy far Eden.
Vain are all disguises! Ah,
Heavenly incognita!
Thy mien bewrayeth through that wrong
The great Uranian House of Song!
As the vintages of earth
Taste of the sun that riped their birth,
We know what never cadent Sun
Thy lamped clusters throbbed upon,
What plumed feet the winepress trod;
Thy wine is flavorous of God.
Whatever singing-robe thou wear
Has the Paradisal air;
And some gold feather it has kept
Shows what Floor it lately swept!

By Reason Of Thy Law

Here I make oath
Although the heart that knows its bitterness
Hear loath,
And credit less
That he who kens to meet Pain's kisses fierce
Which hiss against his tears,
Dread, loss, nor love frustrate,
Nor all iniquity of the froward years
Shall his inur-ed wing make idly bate,
Nor of the appointed quarry his staunch sight
To lose observance quite;
Seal from half-sad and all-elate
Sagacious eyes
Ultimate Paradise;
Nor shake his certitude of haughty fate.

Pacing the burning shares of many dooms,
I with stern tread do the clear-witting stars
To judgment cite,
If I have borne aright
The proving of their pure-willed ordeal.
From food of all delight
The heavenly Falconer my heart debars,
And tames with fearful glooms
The haggard to His call;
Yet sometimes comes a hand, sometimes a voice withal,
And she sits meek now, and expects the light.

In this Avernian sky,
This sultry and incumbent canopy
Of dull and doomed regret;
Where on the unseen verges yet, O yet,
At intervals,
Trembles, and falls,
Faint lightning of remembered transient sweet
Ah, far too sweet
But to be sweet a little, a little sweet, and fleet;
Leaving this pallid trace,
This loitering and most fitful light a space,
Still some sad space,
For Grief to see her own poor face:-

Here where I keep my stand
With all o'er-anguished feet,
And no live comfort near on any hand;
Lo, I proclaim the unavoided term,
When this morass of tears, then drained and firm,
Shall be a land
Unshaken I affirm
Where seven-quired psalterings meet;

And all the gods move with calm hand in hand,
And eyes that know not trouble and the worm.

House Of Bondage

I

When I perceive Love's heavenly reaping still
Regard perforce the clouds' vicissitude,
That the fixed spirit loves not when it will,
But craves its seasons of the flawful blood;
When I perceive that the high poet doth
Oft voiceless stray beneath the uninfluent stars,
That even Urania of her kiss is loath,
And Song's brave wings fret on their sensual bars;
When I perceived the fullest-sail-ed sprite
Lag at most need upon the leth-ed seas,
The provident captainship oft voided quite,
And lam-ed lie deep-draughted argosies;
I scorn myself, that put for such strange toys
The wit of man to purposes of boys.

II

The spirit's ark sealed with a little clay,
Was old ere Memphis grew a memory;
The hand pontifical to break away
That seal what shall surrender? Not the sea
Which did englut great Egypt and his war,
Nor all the desert-drown-ed sepulchres.
Love's feet are stained with clay and travel-sore,
And dusty are Song's lucent wing and hairs.
O Love, that must do courtesy to decay,
Eat hasty bread standing with loins up-girt,
How shall this stead thy feet for their sore way?
Ah, Song, what brief embraces balm thy hurt!
Had Jacob's toil full guerdon, casting his
Twice-seven heaped years to burn in Rachel's kiss?

Ode To The Setting Sun - Prelude

The wailful sweetness of the violin
Floats down the hush-ed waters of the wind,
The heart-strings of the throbbing harp begin
To long in aching music. Spirit-pined,

In wafts that poignant sweetness drifts, until
The wounded soul ooze sadness. The red sun,
A bubble of fire, drops slowly toward the hill,
While one bird prattles that the day is done.

O setting Sun, that as in reverent days
Sinkest in music to thy smooth-ed sleep,

Discrowned of homage, though yet crowned with rays,
Hymned not at harvest more, though reapers reap:

For thee this music wakes not. O deceived,
If thou hear in these thoughtless harmonies
A pious phantom of adorings reaved,
And echo of fair ancient flatteries!

Yet, in this field where the Cross planted reigns,
I know not what strange passion bows my head
To thee, whose great command upon my veins
Proves thee a god for me not dead, not dead!

For worship it is too incredulous,
For doubt oh, too believing-passionate!
What wild divinity makes my heart thus
A fount of most baptismal tears? Thy straight

Long beam lies steady on the Cross. Ah me!
What secret would thy radiant finger show?
Of thy bright mastership is this the key?
Is THIS thy secret, then? And is it woe?

Fling from thine ear the burning curls, and hark
A song thou hast not heard in Northern day;
For Rome too daring, and for Greece too dark,
Sweet with wild wings that pass, that pass away!

The Dread Of Height

Not the Circean wine
Most perilous is for pain:
Grapes of the heavens' star-loaden vine,
Whereto the lofty-placed
Thoughts of fair souls attain,
Tempt with a more retributive delight,
And do disrelish all life's sober taste.
'Tis to have drunk too well
The drink that is divine,
Maketh the kind earth waste,
And breath intolerable.

Ah me!
How shall my mouth content it with mortality?
Lo, secret music, sweetest music,
From distances of distance drifting its lone flight,
Down the arcane where Night would perish in night,
Like a god's loosened locks slips undulously:
Music that is too grievous of the height
For safe and low delight,
Too infinite,

For bounded hearts which yet would girth the sea!

So let it be,
Though sweet be great, and though my heart be small:
So let it be,
O music, music, though you wake in me
No joy, no joy at all;
Although you only wake
Uttermost sadness, measure of delight,
Which else I could not credit to the height,
Did I not know,
That ill is statured to its opposite;
Did I not know,
And even of sadness so,
Of utter sadness make,
Of extreme sad a rod to mete
The incredible excess of unsensed sweet,
And mystic wall of strange felicity.
So let it be,
Though sweet be great, and though my heart be small,
And bitter meat
The food of gods for men to eat;
Yea, John ate daintier, and did tread
Less ways of heat,
Than whom to their wind-carpeted
High banquet-hall,
And golden love-feasts, the fair stars entreat.

But ah withal,
Some hold, some stay,
O difficult Joy, I pray,
Some arms of thine,
Not only, only arms of mine!
Lest like a weary girl I fall
From clasping love so high,
And lacking thus thine arms, then may
Most hapless I
Turn utterly to love of basest rate;
For low they fall whose fall is from the sky.
Yea, who me shall secure
But I of height grown desperate
Surcease my wing, and my lost fate
Be dashed from pure
To broken writhings in the shameful slime:
Lower than man, for I dreamed higher,
Thrust down, by how much I aspire,
And damned with drink of immortality?
For such things be,
Yea, and the lowest reach of reeky Hell
Is but made possible
By forta'en breath of Heaven's austerest clime.

These tidings from the vast to bring
Needeth not doctor nor divine,
Too well, too well
My flesh doth know the heart-perturbing thing;
That dread theology alone
Is mine,
Most native and my own;
And ever with victorious toil
When I have made
Of the deific peaks dim escalade,
My soul with anguish and recoil
Doth like a city in an earthquake rock,
As at my feet the abyss is cloven then,
With deeper menace than for other men,
Of my potential cousinship with mire;
That all my conquered skies do grow a hollow mock,
My fearful powers retire,
No longer strong,
Reversing the shook banners of their song.

Ah, for a heart less native to high Heaven,
A hooded eye, for jesses and restraint,
Or for a will accipitrine to pursue!
The veil of tutelar flesh to simple livers given,
Or those brave-fledging fervours of the Saint,
Whose heavenly falcon-craft doth never taint,
Nor they in sickest time their ample virtue mew.

To The Dead Cardinal Of Westminster

I will not perturbate
Thy Paradisal state
With praise
Of thy dead days;

To the new-heavened say,
'Spirit, thou wert fine clay:'
This do,
Thy praise who knew.

Therefore my spirit clings
Heaven's porter by the wings,
And holds
Its gated golds

Apart, with thee to press
A private business;
Whence,
Deign me audience.

Anchorite, who didst dwell
With all the world for cell
My soul
Round me doth roll

A sequestration bare.
Too far alike we were,
Too far
Dissimilar.

For its burning fruitage I
Do climb the tree o' the sky;
Do prize
Some human eyes.

YOU smelt the Heaven-blossoms,
And all the sweet embosoms
The dear
Uranian year.

Those Eyes my weak gaze shuns,
Which to the suns are Suns.
Did
Not affray your lid.

The carpet was let down
(With golden mouldings strown)
For you
Of the angels' blue.

But I, ex-Paradised,
The shoulder of your Christ
Find high
To lean thereby.

So flaps my helpless sail,
Bellying with neither gale,
Of Heaven
Nor Orcus even.

Life is a coquetry
Of Death, which wearies me,
Too sure
Of the amour;

A tiring-room where I
Death's divers garments try,
Till fit
Some fashion sit.

It seemeth me too much

I do rehearse for such
A mean
And single scene.

The sandy glass hence bear
Antique remembrancer;
My veins
Do spare its pains.

With secret sympathy
My thoughts repeat in me
Infirm
The turn o' the worm

Beneath my appointed sod:
The grave is in my blood;
I shake
To winds that take

Its grasses by the top;
The rains thereon that drop
Perturb
With drip acerb

My subtly answering soul;
The feet across its knoll
Do jar
Me from afar.

As sap foretastes the spring;
As Earth ere blossoming
Thrills
With far daffodils,

And feels her breast turn sweet
With the unconceived wheat;
So doth
My flesh foreloathe

The abhorred spring of Dis,
With seething presciences
Affirm
The preparate worm.

I have no thought that I,
When at the last I die,
Shall reach
To gain your speech.

But you, should that be so,
May very well, I know,

May well
To me in hell

With recognising eyes
Look from your Paradise -
'God bless
Thy hopelessness!'

Call, holy soul, O call
The hosts angelical,
And say,
'See, far away

'Lies one I saw on earth;
One stricken from his birth
With curse
Of destinate verse.

'What place doth He ye serve
For such sad spirit reserve,
Given,
In dark lieu of Heaven,

'The impitiable Daemon,
Beauty, to adore and dream on,
To be
Perpetually

'Hers, but she never his?
He reapeth miseries,
Foreknows
His wages woes;

'He lives detached days;
He serveth not for praise;
For gold
He is not sold;

'Deaf is he to world's tongue;
He scorneth for his song
The loud
Shouts of the crowd;

'He asketh not world's eyes;
Not to world's ears he cries;
Saith, 'These
Shut, if ye please;'

'He measureth world's pleasure,
World's ease as Saints might measure;
For hire

Just love entire

'He asks, not grudging pain;
And knows his asking vain,
And cries
'Love! Love!' and dies;

'In guerdon of long duty,
Unowned by Love or Beauty;
And goes -
Tell, tell, who knows!

'Aliens from Heaven's worth,
Fine beasts who nose i' the earth,
Do there
Reward prepare.

'But are HIS great desires
Food but for nether fires?
Ah me,
A mystery!

'Can it be his alone,
To find when all is known,
That what
He solely sought

'Is lost, and thereto lost
All that its seeking cost?
That he
Must finally,

'Through sacrificial tears,
And anchoretic years,
Tryst
With the sensualist?'

So ask; and if they tell
The secret terrible,
Good friend,
I pray thee send

Some high gold embassage
To teach my unripe age.
Tell!
Lest my feet walk hell.

Dedication To Coventry Patmore.

Lo, my book thinks to look Time's leaguer down,
Under the banner of your spread renown!

Or if these levies of impuissant rhyme
Fall to the overthrow of assaulting Time,
Yet this one page shall fend oblivious shame,
Armed with your crested and prevailing Name.

Dedication To Wilfred And Alice Meynell

If the rose in meek duty
May dedicate humbly
To her grower the beauty
Wherewith she is comely;
If the mine to the miner
The jewels that pined in it,
Earth to diviner
The springs he divined in it;
To the grapes the wine-pitcher
Their juice that was crushed in it,
Viol to its witcher
The music lay hushed in it;
If the lips may pay Gladness
In laughters she wakened,
And the heart to its sadness
Weeping unslakened,
If the hid and sealed coffer,
Whose having not his is,
To the loosers may proffer
Their finding, here this is;
Their lives if all livers
To the Life of all living,
To you, O dear givers!
I give your own giving.

The Kingdom Of God

'In no Strange Land'

O world invisible, we view thee,
O world intangible, we touch thee,
O world unknowable, we know thee,
Inapprehensible, we clutch thee!

Does the fish soar to find the ocean,
The eagle plunge to find the air
That we ask of the stars in motion
If they have rumour of thee there?

Not where the wheeling systems darken,
And our benumbed conceiving soars!
The drift of pinions, would we hearken,
Beats at our own clay-shuttered doors.

The angels keep their ancient places;
Turn but a stone, and start a wing!
'Tis ye, 'tis your estranged faces,
That miss the many-splendoured thing.

But (when so sad thou canst not sadder)
Cry; and upon thy so sore loss
Shall shine the traffic of Jacob's ladder
Pitched betwixt Heaven and Charing Cross.

Yea, in the night, my Soul, my daughter,
Cry, clinging Heaven by the hems;
And lo, Christ walking on the water
Not of Gennesareth, but Thames!

Sister Songs - An Offering To Two Sisters - The Proem

Shrewd winds and shrill were these the speech of May?
A ragged, slag-grey sky invested so,
Mary's spoilt nursling! wert thou wont to go?
Or THOU, Sun-god and song-god, say
Could singer pipe one tiniest linnet-lay,
While Song did turn away his face from song?
Or who could be
In spirit or in body hale for long,
Old AEsculap's best Master! lacking thee?
At length, then, thou art here!
On the earth's lethed ear
Thy voice of light rings out exultant, strong;
Through dreams she stirs and murmurs at that summons dear:
From its red leash my heart strains tamelessly,
For Spring leaps in the womb of the young year!
Nay, was it not brought forth before,
And we waited, to behold it,
Till the sun's hand should unfold it,
What the year's young bosom bore?
Even so; it came, nor knew we that it came,
In the sun's eclipse.
Yet the birds have plighted vows,
And from the branches pipe each other's name;
Yet the season all the boughs
Has kindled to the finger-tips,
Mark yonder, how the long laburnum drips
Its jocund spilth of fire, its honey of wild flame!
Yea, and myself put on swift quickening,
And answer to the presence of a sudden Spring.
From cloud-zoned pinnacles of the secret spirit
Song falls precipitant in dizzying streams;
And, like a mountain-hold when war-shouts stir it,
The mind's recessed fastness casts to light
Its gleaming multitudes, that from every height

Unfurl the flaming of a thousand dreams.
Now therefore, thou who bring'st the year to birth,
Who guid'st the bare and dabbled feet of May;
Sweet stem to that rose Christ, who from the earth
Suck'st our poor prayers, conveying them to Him;
Be aidant, tender Lady, to my lay!
Of thy two maidens somewhat must I say,
Ere shadowy twilight lashes, drooping, dim
Day's dreamy eyes from us;
Ere eve has struck and furled
The beamy-textured tent transpicuous,
Of webbed coerule wrought and woven calms,
Whence has paced forth the lambent-footed sun.
And Thou disclose my flower of song upcurled,
Who from Thy fair irradiant palms
Scatterest all love and loveliness as alms;
Yea, Holy One,
Who coin'st Thyself to beauty for the world!

Then, Spring's little children, your lauds do ye upraise
To Sylvia, O Sylvia, her sweet, feat ways!
Your lovesome labours lay away,
And trick you out in holiday,
For syllabling to Sylvia;
And all you birds on branches, lave your mouths with May,
To bear with me this burthen,
For singing to Sylvia.

Sister Songs - An Offering To Two Sisters - Part The First

The leaves dance, the leaves sing,
The leaves dance in the breath of the Spring.
I bid them dance,
I bid them sing,
For the limpid glance
Of my ladyling;
For the gift to the Spring of a dewier spring,
For God's good grace of this ladyling!
I know in the lane, by the hedgerow track,
The long, broad grasses underneath
Are warted with rain like a toad's knobbed back;
But here May weareth a rainless wreath.
In the new-sucked milk of the sun's bosom
Is dabbled the mouth of the daisy-blossom;
The smouldering rosebud chars through its sheath;
The lily stirs her snowy limbs,
Ere she swims
Naked up through her cloven green,
Like the wave-born Lady of Love Hellene;
And the scattered snowdrop exquisite
Twinkles and gleams,

As if the showers of the sunny beams
Were splashed from the earth in drops of light.
Everything
That is child of Spring
Casts its bud or blossoming
Upon the stream of my delight.

Their voices, that scents are, now let them upraise
To Sylvia, O Sylvia, her sweet, feat ways!
Their lovely mother them array,
And prank them out in holiday,
For syllabling to Sylvia;
And all the birds on branches lave their mouths with May,
To bear with me this burthen,
For singing to Sylvia.

2.
While thus I stood in mazes bound
Of vernal sorcery,
I heard a dainty dubious sound,
As of goodly melody;
Which first was faint as if in swound,
Then burst so suddenly
In warring concord all around,
That, whence this thing might be,
To see
The very marrow longed in me!
It seemed of air, it seemed of ground,
And never any witchery
Drawn from pipe, or reed, or string,
Made such dulcet ravishing.
'Twas like no earthly instrument,
Yet had something of them all
In its rise, and in its fall;
As if in one sweet consort there were blent
Those archetypes celestial
Which our endeavouring instruments recall.
So heavenly flutes made murmurous plain
To heavenly viols, that again
Aching with music wailed back pain;
Regals release their notes, which rise
Welling, like tears from heart to eyes;
And the harp thrills with thronging sighs.
Horns in mellow flattering
Parley with the cithern-string:-
Hark! the floating, long-drawn note
Woos the throbbing cithern-string!

Their pretty, pretty prating those citherns sure upraise
For homage unto Sylvia, her sweet, feat ways:
Those flutes do flute their vowelled lay,

Their lovely languid language say,
For lisping to Sylvia;
Those viols' lissom bowings break the heart of May,
And harps harp their burthen,
For singing to Sylvia.

3.
Now at that music and that mirth
Rose, as 'twere, veils from earth;
And I spied
How beside
Bud, bell, bloom, an elf
Stood, or was the flower itself
'Mid radiant air
All the fair
Frequence swayed in irised wavers.
Some against the gleaming rims
Their bosoms prest
Of the kingcups, to the brims
Filled with sun, and their white limbs
Bathed in those golden lavers;
Some on the brown, glowing breast
Of that Indian maid, the pansy,
(Through its tenuous veils confest
Of swathing light), in a quaint fancy
Tied her knot of yellow favours;
Others dared open draw
Snapdragon's dreadful jaw:
Some, just sprung from out the soil,
Sleeked and shook their rumpled fans
Dropt with sheen
Of moony green;
Others, not yet extricate,
On their hands leaned their weight,
And writhed them free with mickle toil,
Still folded in their veiny vans:
And all with an unsought accord
Sang together from the sward;
Whence had come, and from sprites
Yet unseen, those delights,
As of tempered musics blent,
Which had given me such content.
For haply our best instrument,
Pipe or cithern, stopped or strung,
Mimics but some spirit tongue.

Their amiable voices, I bid them upraise
To Sylvia, O Sylvia, her sweet, feat ways;
Their lovesome labours laid away,
To linger out this holiday
In syllabling to Sylvia;

While all the birds on branches lave their mouths with May,
To bear with me this burthen,
For singing to Sylvia.

4.
Next I saw, wonder-whist,
How from the atmosphere a mist,
So it seemed, slow uprist;
And, looking from those elfin swarms,
I was 'ware
How the air
Was all populous with forms
Of the Hours, floating down,
Like Nereids through a watery town.
Some, with languors of waved arms,
Fluctuous oared their flexile way;
Some were borne half resupine
On the aerial hyaline,
Their fluid limbs and rare array
Flickering on the wind, as quivers
Trailing weed in running rivers;
And others, in far prospect seen,
Newly loosed on this terrene,
Shot in piercing swiftness came,
With hair a-stream like pale and goblin flame.
As crystelline ice in water,
Lay in air each faint daughter;
Inseparate (or but separate dim)
Circumfused wind from wind-like vest,
Wind-like vest from wind-like limb.
But outward from each lucid breast,
When some passion left its haunt,
Radiate surge of colour came,
Diffusing blush-wise, palpitant,
Dying all the filmy frame.
With some sweet tenderness they would
Turn to an amber-clear and glossy gold;
Or a fine sorrow, lovely to behold,
Would sweep them as the sun and wind's joined flood
Sweeps a greening-sapphire sea;
Or they would glow enamouredly
Illustrious sanguine, like a grape of blood;
Or with mantling poetry
Curd to the tincture which the opal hath,
Like rainbows thawing in a moonbeam bath.
So paled they, flushed they, swam they, sang melodiously.

Their chanting, soon fading, let them, too, upraise
For homage unto Sylvia, her sweet, feat ways;
Weave with suave float their waved way,
And colours take of holiday,

For syllabling to Sylvia;
And all the birds on branches lave their mouths with May,
To bear with me this burthen,
For singing to Sylvia.

5.
Then, through those translucencies,
As grew my senses clearer clear,
Did I see, and did I hear,
How under an elm's canopy
Wheeled a flight of Dryades
Murmuring measured melody.
Gyre in gyre their treading was,
Wheeling with an adverse flight,
In twi-circle o'er the grass,
These to left, and those to right;
All the band
Linked by each other's hand;
Decked in raiment stained as
The blue-helmed aconite.
And they advance with flutter, with grace,
To the dance
Moving on with a dainty pace,
As blossoms mince it on river swells.
Over their heads their cymbals shine,
Round each ankle gleams a twine
Of twinkling bells -
Tune twirled golden from their cells.
Every step was a tinkling sound,
As they glanced in their dancing-ground,
Clouds in cluster with such a sailing
Float o'er the light of the wasting moon,
As the cloud of their gliding veiling
Swung in the sway of the dancing-tune.
There was the clash of their cymbals clanging,
Ringing of swinging bells clinging their feet;
And the clang on wing it seemed a-hanging,
Hovering round their dancing so fleet.
I stirred, I rustled more than meet;
Whereat they broke to the left and right,
With eddying robes like aconite
Blue of helm;
And I beheld to the foot o' the elm.

They have not tripped those dances, betrayed to my gaze,
To glad the heart of Sylvia, beholding of their maze;
Through barky walls have slid away,
And tricked them in their holiday,
For other than for Sylvia;
While all the birds on branches lave their mouths with May,
And bear with me this burthen,

For singing to Sylvia.

6.
Where its umbrage was enrooted,
Sat white-suited,
Sat green-amiced, and bare-footed,
Spring amid her minstrelsy;
There she sat amid her ladies,
Where the shade is
Sheen as Enna mead ere Hades'
Gloom fell thwart Persephone.
Dewy buds were interstrown
Through her tresses hanging down,
And her feet
Were most sweet,
Tinged like sea-stars, rosied brown.
A throng of children like to flowers were sown
About the grass beside, or clomb her knee:
I looked who were that favoured company.
And one there stood
Against the beamy flood
Of sinking day, which, pouring its abundance,
Sublimed the illuminous and volute redundance
Of locks that, half dissolving, floated round her face;
As see I might
Far off a lily-cluster poised in sun
Dispread its gracile curls of light
I knew what chosen child was there in place!
I knew there might no brows be, save of one,
With such Hesperian fulgence compassed,
Which in her moving seemed to wheel about her head.

O Spring's little children, more loud your lauds upraise,
For this is even Sylvia, with her sweet, feat ways!
Your lovesome labours lay away,
And prank you out in holiday,
For syllabling to Sylvia;
And all you birds on branches, lave your mouths with May,
To bear with me this burthen
For singing to Sylvia!

7.
Spring, goddess, is it thou, desired long?
And art thou girded round with this young train? -
If ever I did do thee ease in song,
Now of thy grace let me one meed obtain,
And list thou to one plain.
Oh, keep still in thy train
After the years when others therefrom fade,
This tiny, well-belovèd maid!
To whom the gate of my heart's fortalice,

With all which in it is,
And the shy self who doth therein immew him
'Gainst what loud leagurers battailously woo him,
I, bribed traitor to him,
Set open for one kiss.

Then suffer, Spring, thy children, that lauds they should upraise
To Sylvia, this Sylvia, her sweet, feat ways;
Their lovely labours lay away,
And trick them out in holiday,
For syllabling to Sylvia;
And that all birds on branches lave their mouths with May,
To bear with me this burthen,
For singing to Sylvia.

8.
A kiss? for a child's kiss?
Aye, goddess, even for this.
Once, bright Sylviola! in days not far,
Once in that nightmare-time which still doth haunt
My dreams, a grim, unbidden visitant
Forlorn, and faint, and stark,
I had endured through watches of the dark
The abashless inquisition of each star,
Yea, was the outcast mark
Of all those heavenly passers' scrutiny;
Stood bound and helplessly
For Time to shoot his barbed minutes at me;
Suffered the trampling hoof of every hour
In night's slow-wheeled car;
Until the tardy dawn dragged me at length
From under those dread wheels; and, bled of strength,
I waited the inevitable last.
Then there came past
A child; like thee, a spring-flower; but a flower
Fallen from the budded coronal of Spring,
And through the city-streets blown withering.
She passed, O brave, sad, lovingest, tender thing! -
And of her own scant pittance did she give,
That I might eat and live:
Then fled, a swift and trackless fugitive.
Therefore I kissed in thee
The heart of Childhood, so divine for me;
And her, through what sore ways,
And what unchildish days,
Borne from me now, as then, a trackless fugitive.
Therefore I kissed in thee
Her, child! and innocency,
And spring, and all things that have gone from me,
And that shall never be;
All vanished hopes, and all most hopeless bliss,

Came with thee to my kiss.
And ah! so long myself had strayed afar
From child, and woman, and the boon earth's green,
And all wherewith life's face is fair beseen;
Journeying its journey bare
Five suns, except of the all-kissing sun
Unkissed of one;
Almost I had forgot
The healing harms,
And whitest witchery, a-lurk in that
Authentic cestus of two girdling arms:
And I remembered not
The subtle sanctities which dart
From childish lips' unvalued precious brush,
Nor how it makes the sudden lilies push
Between the loosening fibres of the heart.
Then, that thy little kiss
Should be to me all this,
Let workaday wisdom blink sage lids thereat;
Which towers a flight three hedgerows high, poor bat!
And straightway charts me out the empyreal air.
Its chart I wing not by, its canon of worth
Scorn not, nor reck though mine should breed it mirth:
And howso thou and I may be disjoint,
Yet still my falcon spirit makes her point
Over the covert where
Thou, sweetest quarry, hast put in from her!

(Soul, hush these sad numbers, too sad to upraise
In hymning bright Sylvia, unlearn'd in such ways!
Our mournful moods lay we away,
And prank our thoughts in holiday,
For syllabling to Sylvia;
When all the birds on branches lave their mouths with May,
To bear with us this burthen,
For singing to Sylvia!)

9.
Then thus Spring, bounteous lady, made reply:
O lover of me and all my progeny,
For grace to you
I take her ever to my retinue.
Over thy form, dear child, alas! my art
Cannot prevail; but mine immortalising
Touch I lay upon thy heart.
Thy soul's fair shape
In my unfading mantle's green I drape,
And thy white mind shall rest by my devising
A Gideon-fleece amid life's dusty drouth.
If Even burst yon globed yellow grape
(Which is the sun to mortals' sealed sight)

Against her stained mouth;
Or if white-handed light
Draw thee yet dripping from the quiet pools,
Still lucencies and cools,
Of sleep, which all night mirror constellate dreams;
Like to the sign which led the Israelite,
Thy soul, through day or dark,
A visible brightness on the chosen ark
Of thy sweet body and pure,
Shall it assure,
With auspice large and tutelary gleams,
Appointed solemn courts, and covenanted streams.'

Cease, Spring's little children, now cease your lauds to raise;
That dream is past, and Sylvia, with her sweet, feat ways.
Our loved labour, laid away,
Is smoothly ended; said our say,
Our syllable to Sylvia.
Make sweet, you birds on branches! make sweet your mouths with May!
But borne is this burthen,
Sung unto Sylvia.

Sister Songs - An Offering To Two Sisters - Part The Second

And now, thou elder nursling of the nest;
Ere all the intertangled west
Be one magnificence
Of multitudinous blossoms that o'errun
The flaming brazen bowl o' the burnished sun
Which they do flower from,
How shall I 'stablish THY memorial?
Nay, how or with what countenance shall I come
To plead in my defence
For loving thee at all?
I who can scarcely speak my fellows' speech,
Love their love, or mine own love to them teach;
A bastard barred from their inheritance,
Who seem, in this dim shape's uneasy nook,
Some sun-flower's spirit which by luckless chance
Has mournfully its tenement mistook;
When it were better in its right abode,
Heartless and happy lackeying its god.
How com'st thou, little tender thing of white,
Whose very touch full scantly me beseems,
How com'st thou resting on my vaporous dreams,
Kindling a wraith there of earth's vernal green?
Even so as I have seen,
In night's aerial sea with no wind blust'rous,
A ribbed tract of cloudy malachite
Curve a shored crescent wide;

And on its slope marge shelving to the night
The stranded moon lay quivering like a lustrous
Medusa newly washed up from the tide,
Lay in an oozy pool of its own deliquious light.

Yet hear how my excuses may prevail,
Nor, tender white orb, be thou opposite!
Life and life's beauty only hold their revels
In the abysmal ocean's luminous levels.
There, like the phantasms of a poet pale,
The exquisite marvels sail:
Clarified silver; greens and azures frail
As if the colours sighed themselves away,
And blent in supersubtile interplay
As if they swooned into each other's arms;
Repured vermilion,
Like ear-tips 'gainst the sun;
And beings that, under night's swart pinion,
Make every wave upon the harbour-bars
A beaten yolk of stars.
But where day's glance turns baffled from the deeps,
Die out those lovely swarms;
And in the immense profound no creature glides or creeps.

Love and love's beauty only hold their revels
In life's familiar, penetrable levels:
What of its ocean-floor?
I dwell there evermore.
From almost earliest youth
I raised the lids o' the truth,
And forced her bend on me her shrinking sight;
Ever I knew me Beauty's eremite,
In antre of this lowly body set.
Girt with a thirsty solitude of soul.
Nathless I not forget
How I have, even as the anchorite,
I too, imperishing essences that console.
Under my ruined passions, fallen and sere,
The wild dreams stir like little radiant girls,
Whom in the moulted plumage of the year
Their comrades sweet have buried to the curls.
Yet, though their dedicated amorist,
How often do I bid my visions hist,
Deaf to them, pleading all their piteous fills;
Who weep, as weep the maidens of the mist
Clinging the necks of the unheeding hills:
And their tears wash them lovelier than before,
That from grief's self our sad delight grows more,
Fair are the soul's uncrisped calms, indeed,
Endiapered with many a spiritual form
Of blosmy-tinctured weed;

But scarce itself is conscious of the store
Suckled by it, and only after storm
Casts up its loosened thoughts upon the shore.
To this end my deeps are stirred;
And I deem well why life unshared
Was ordained me of yore.
In pairing-time, we know, the bird
Kindles to its deepmost splendour,
And the tender
Voice is tenderest in its throat;
Were its love, for ever nigh it,
Never by it,
It might keep a vernal note,
The crocean and amethystine
In their pristine
Lustre linger on its coat.
Therefore must my song-bower lone be,
That my tone be
Fresh with dewy pain alway;
She, who scorns my dearest care ta'en,
An uncertain
Shadow of the sprite of May.
And is my song sweet, as they say?
Tis sweet for one whose voice has no reply,
Save silence's sad cry:
And are its plumes a burning bright array?
They burn for an unincarnated eye
A bubble, charioteered by the inward breath
Which, ardorous for its own invisible lure,
Urges me glittering to aerial death,
I am rapt towards that bodiless paramour;
Blindly the uncomprehended tyranny
Obeying of my heart's impetuous might.
The earth and all its planetary kin,
Starry buds tangled in the whirling hair
That flames round the Phoebean wassailer,
Speed no more ignorant, more predestined flight,
Than I, HER viewless tresses netted in.
As some most beautiful one, with lovely taunting,
Her eyes of guileless guile o'ercanopies,
Does her hid visage bow,
And miserly your covetous gaze allow,
By inchmeal, coy degrees,
Saying 'Can you see me now?'
Yet from the mouth's reflex you guess the wanting
Smile of the coming eyes
In all their upturned grievous witcheries,
Before that sunbreak rise;
And each still hidden feature view within
Your mind, as eager scrutinies detail
The moon's young rondure through the shamefast veil

Drawn to her gleaming chin:
After this wise,
From the enticing smile of earth and skies
I dream my unknown Fair's refused gaze;
And guessingly her love's close traits devise,
Which she with subtile coquetries
Through little human glimpses slow displays,
Cozening my mateless days
By sick, intolerable delays.
And so I keep mine uncompanioned ways;
And so my touch, to golden poesies
Turning love's bread, is bought at hunger's price.
So, in the inextinguishable wars
Which roll song's Orient on the sullen night
Whose ragged banners in their own despite
Take on the tinges of the hated light, -
So Sultan Phoebus has his Janizars.
But if mine unappeased cicatrices
Might get them lawful ease;
Were any gentle passion hallowed me,
Who must none other breath of passion feel
Save such as winnows to the fledged heel
The tremulous Paradisal plumages;
The conscious sacramental trees
Which ever be
Shaken celestially,
Consentient with enamoured wings, might know my love for thee.
Yet is there more, whereat none guesseth, love!
Upon the ending of my deadly night
(Whereof thou hast not the surmise, and slight
Is all that any mortal knows thereof),
Thou wert to me that earnest of day's light,
When, like the back of a gold-mailed saurian
Heaving its slow length from Nilotic slime,
The first long gleaming fissure runs Aurorian
Athwart the yet dun firmament of prime.
Stretched on the margin of the cruel sea
Whence they had rescued me,
With faint and painful pulses was I lying;
Not yet discerning well
If I had 'scaped, or were an icicle,
Whose thawing is its dying.
Like one who sweats before a despot's gate,
Summoned by some presaging scroll of fate,
And knows not whether kiss or dagger wait;
And all so sickened is his countenance,
The courtiers buzz, 'Lo, doomed!' and look at him askance:-
At Fate's dread portal then
Even so stood I, I ken,
Even so stood I, between a joy and fear,
And said to mine own heart, 'Now if the end be here!'

They say, Earth's beauty seems completest
To them that on their death-beds rest;
Gentle lady! she smiles sweetest
Just ere she clasp us to her breast.
And I, now MY Earth's countenance grew bright,
Did she but smile me towards that nuptial-night?
But whileas on such dubious bed I lay,
One unforgotten day,
As a sick child waking sees
Wide-eyed daisies
Gazing on it from its hand,
Slipped there for its dear amazes;
So between thy father's knees
I saw THEE stand,
And through my hazes
Of pain and fear thine eyes' young wonder shone.
Then, as flies scatter from a carrion,
Or rooks in spreading gyres like broken smoke
Wheel, when some sound their quietude has broke,
Fled, at thy countenance, all that doubting spawn:
The heart which I had questioned spoke,
A cry impetuous from its depths was drawn, -
'I take the omen of this face of dawn!'
And with the omen to my heart cam'st thou.
Even with a spray of tears
That one light draft was fixed there for the years.

And now?
The hours I tread ooze memories of thee, Sweet!
Beneath my casual feet.
With rainfall as the lea,
The day is drenched with thee;
In little exquisite surprises
Bubbling deliciousness of thee arises
From sudden places,
Under the common traces
Of my most lethargied and customed paces.

As an Arab journeyeth
Through a sand of Ayaman,
Lean Thirst, lolling its cracked tongue,
Lagging by his side along;
And a rusty-winged Death
Grating its low flight before,
Casting ribbed shadows o'er
The blank desert, blank and tan:
He lifts by hap toward where the morning's roots are
His weary stare,
Sees, although they plashless mutes are,
Set in a silver air

Fountains of gelid shoots are,
Making the daylight fairest fair;
Sees the palm and tamarind
Tangle the tresses of a phantom wind; -
A sight like innocence when one has sinned!
A green and maiden freshness smiling there,
While with unblinking glare
The tawny-hided desert crouches watching her.

'Tis a vision:
Yet the greeneries Elysian
He has known in tracts afar;
Thus the enamouring fountains flow,
Those the very palms that grow,
By rare-gummed Sava, or Herbalimar.

Such a watered dream has tarried
Trembling on my desert arid;
Even so
Its lovely gleamings
Seemings show
Of things not seemings;
And I gaze,
Knowing that, beyond my ways,
Verily
All these ARE, for these are she.
Eve no gentlier lays her cooling cheek
On the burning brow of the sick earth,
Sick with death, and sick with birth,
Aeon to aeon, in secular fever twirled,
Than thy shadow soothes this weak
And distempered being of mine.
In all I work, my hand includeth thine;
Thou rushest down in every stream
Whose passion frets my spirit's deepening gorge;
Unhood'st mine eyas-heart, and fliest my dream;
Thou swing'st the hammers of my forge;
As the innocent moon, that nothing does but shine,
Moves all the labouring surges of the world.
Pierce where thou wilt the springing thought in me,
And there thy pictured countenance lies enfurled,
As in the cut fern lies the imaged tree.
This poor song that sings of thee,
This fragile song, is but a curled
Shell outgathered from thy sea,
And murmurous still of its nativity.
Princess of Smiles!
Sorceress of most unlawful-lawful wiles!
Cunning pit for gazers' senses,
Overstrewn with innocences!
Purities gleam white like statues

In the fair lakes of thine eyes,
And I watch the sparkles that use
There to rise,
Knowing these
Are bubbles from the calyces
Of the lovely thoughts that breathe
Paving, like water-flowers, thy spirit's floor beneath.

O thou most dear!
Who art thy sex's complex harmony
God-set more facilely;
To thee may love draw near
Without one blame or fear,
Unchidden save by his humility:
Thou Perseus' Shield! wherein I view secure
The mirrored Woman's fateful-fair allure!
Whom Heaven still leaves a twofold dignity,
As girlhood gentle, and as boyhood free;
With whom no most diaphanous webs enwind
The bared limbs of the rebukeless mind.
Wild Dryad! all unconscious of thy tree,
With which indissolubly
The tyrannous time shall one day make thee whole;
Whose frank arms pass unfretted through its bole:
Who wear'st thy femineity
Light as entrailed blossoms, that shalt find
It erelong silver shackles unto thee.
Thou whose young sex is yet but in thy soul;
As hoarded in the vine
Hang the gold skins of undelirious wine,
As air sleeps, till it toss its limbs in breeze:-
In whom the mystery which lures and sunders,
Grapples and thrusts apart; endears, estranges;
- The dragon to its own Hesperides -
Is gated under slow-revolving changes,
Manifold doors of heavy-hinged years.
So once, ere Heaven's eyes were filled with wonders
To see Laughter rise from Tears,
Lay in beauty not yet mighty,
Conched in translucencies,
The antenatal Aphrodite,
Caved magically under magic seas;
Caved dreamlessly beneath the dreamful seas.

'Whose sex is in thy soul!'
What think we of thy soul?
Which has no parts, and cannot grow,
Unfurled not from an embryo;
Born of full stature, lineal to control;
And yet a pigmy's yoke must undergo.
Yet must keep pace and tarry, patient, kind,

With its unwilling scholar, the dull, tardy mind;
Must be obsequious to the body's powers,
Whose low hands mete its paths, set ope and close its ways;
Must do obeisance to the days,
And wait the little pleasure of the hours;
Yea, ripe for kingship, yet must be
Captive in statuted minority!
So is all power fulfilled, as soul in thee.
So still the ruler by the ruled takes rule,
And wisdom weaves itself i' the loom o' the fool.
The splendent sun no splendour can display,
Till on gross things he dash his broken ray,
From cloud and tree and flower re-tossed in prismy spray.
Did not obstruction's vessel hem it in,
Force were not force, would spill itself in vain
We know the Titan by his champed chain.
Stay is heat's cradle, it is rocked therein,
And by check's hand is burnished into light;
If hate were none, would love burn lowlier bright?
God's Fair were guessed scarce but for opposite sin;
Yea, and His Mercy, I do think it well,
Is flashed back from the brazen gates of Hell.
The heavens decree
All power fulfil itself as soul in thee.
For supreme Spirit subject was to clay,
And Law from its own servants learned a law,
And Light besought a lamp unto its way,
And Awe was reined in awe,
At one small house of Nazareth;
And Golgotha
Saw Breath to breathlessness resign its breath,
And Life do homage for its crown to death.

So is all power, as soul in thee increased!
But, knowing this, in knowledge's despite
I fret against the law severe that stains
Thy spirit with eclipse;
When as a nymph's carven head sweet water drips,
For others oozing so the cool delight
Which cannot steep her stiffened mouth of stone
Thy nescient lips repeat maternal strains.
Memnonian lips!
Smitten with singing from thy mother's east,
And murmurous with music not their own:
Nay, the lips flexile, while the mind alone
A passionless statue stands.
Oh, pardon, innocent one!
Pardon at thine unconscious hands!
'Murmurous with music not their own,' I say?
And in that saying how do I missay,
When from the common sands

Of poorest common speech of common day
Thine accents sift the golden musics out!
And ah, we poets, I misdoubt,
Are little more than thou!
We speak a lesson taught we know not how,
And what it is that from us flows
The hearer better than the utterer knows.

Thou canst foreshape thy word;
The poet is not lord
Of the next syllable may come
With the returning pendulum;
And what he plans to-day in song,
To-morrow sings it in another tongue.
Where the last leaf fell from his bough,
He knows not if a leaf shall grow,
Where he sows he doth not reap,
He reapeth where he did not sow;
He sleeps, and dreams forsake his sleep
To meet him on his waking way.
Vision will mate him not by law and vow:
Disguised in life's most hodden-grey,
By the most beaten road of everyday
She waits him, unsuspected and unknown.
The hardest pang whereon
He lays his mutinous head may be a Jacob's stone.
In the most iron crag his foot can tread
A Dream may strew her bed,
And suddenly his limbs entwine,
And draw him down through rock as sea-nymphs might through brine.
But, unlike those feigned temptress-ladies who
In guerdon of a night the lover slew,
When the embrace has failed, the rapture fled,
Not he, not he, the wild sweet witch is dead!
And, though he cherisheth
The babe most strangely born from out her death,
Some tender trick of her it hath, maybe,
It is not she!

Yet, even as the air is rumorous of fray
Before the first shafts of the sun's onslaught
From gloom's black harness splinter,
And Summer move on Winter
With the trumpet of the March, and the pennon of the May;
As gesture outstrips thought;
So, haply, toyer with ethereal strings!
Are thy blind repetitions of high things
The murmurous gnats whose aimless hoverings
Reveal song's summer in the air;
The outstretched hand, which cannot thought declare,
Yet is thought's harbinger.

These strains the way for thine own strains prepare;
We feel the music moist upon this breeze,
And hope the congregating poesies.
Sundered yet by thee from us
Wait, with wild eyes luminous,
All thy winged things that are to be;
They flit against thee, Gate of Ivory!
They clamour on the portress Destiny,
'Set her wide, so we may issue through!
Our vans are quick for that they have to do
Suffer still your young desire;
Your plumes but bicker at the tips with fire,
Tarry their kindling; they will beat the higher.
And thou, bright girl, not long shalt thou repeat
Idly the music from thy mother caught;
Not vainly has she wrought,
Not vainly from the cloudward-jetting turret
Of her aerial mind, for thy weak feet,
Let down the silken ladder of her thought.
She bare thee with a double pain,
Of the body and the spirit;
Thou thy fleshly weeds hast ta'en,
Thy diviner weeds inherit!
The precious streams which through thy young lips roll
Shall leave their lovely delta in thy soul:
Where sprites of so essential kind
Set their paces,
Surely they shall leave behind
The green traces
Of their sportance in the mind,
And thou shalt, ere we well may know it,
Turn that daintiness, a poet,
Elfin-ring
Where sweet fancies foot and sing.
So it may be, so it SHALL be,
Oh, take the prophecy from me!
What if the old fastidious sculptor, Time,
This crescent marvel of his hands
Carveth all too painfully,
And I who prophesy shall never see?
What if the niche of its predestined rhyme,
Its aching niche, too long expectant stands?
Yet shall he after sore delays
On some exultant day of days
The white enshrouding childhood raise
From thy fair spirit, finished for our gaze;
While we (but 'mongst that happy 'we'
The prophet cannot be!)
While we behold with no astonishments,
With that serene fulfilment of delight
Wherewith we view the sight

When the stars pitch the golden tents
Of their high campment on the plains of night.
Why should amazement be our satellite?
What wonder in such things?
If angels have hereditary wings,
If not by Salic law is handed down
The poet's crown,
To thee, born in the purple of the throne,
The laurel must belong:
Thou, in thy mother's right
Descendant of Castalian-chrismed kings
O Princess of the Blood of Song!

Peace; too impetuously have I been winging
Toward vaporous heights which beckon and beguile
I sink back, saddened to my inmost mind;
Even as I list a-dream that mother singing
The poesy of sweet tone, and sadden, while
Her voice is cast in troubled wake behind
The keel of her keen spirit. Thou art enshrined
In a too primal innocence for this eye
Intent on such untempered radiancy
Not to be pained; my clay can scarce endure
Ungrieved the effluence near of essences so pure.
Therefore, little, tender maiden,
Never be thou overshaden
With a mind whose canopy
Would shut out the sky from thee;
Whose tangled branches intercept Heaven's light:
I will not feed my unpastured heart
On thee, green pleasaunce as thou art,
To lessen by one flower thy happy daisies white.
The water-rat is earth-hued like the runlet
Whereon he swims; and how in me should lurk
Thoughts apt to neighbour thine, thou creature sunlit?
If through long fret and irk
Thine eyes within their browed recesses were
Worn caves where thought lay couchant in its lair;
Wert thou a spark among dank leaves, ah ruth!
With age in all thy veins, while all thy heart was youth;
Our contact might run smooth.
But life's Eoan dews still moist thy ringed hair;
Dian's chill finger-tips
Thaw if at night they happen on thy lips;
The flying fringes of the sun's cloak frush
The fragile leaves which on those warm lips blush;
And joy only lurks retired
In the dim gloaming of thine irid.
Then since my love drags this poor shadow, me,
And one without the other may not be,
From both I guard thee free.

It still is much, yes, it is much,
Only my dream! to love my love of thee;
And it is much, yes, it is much,
In hands which thou hast touched to feel thy touch
In voices which have mingled with thine own
To hear a double tone.
As anguish, for supreme expression prest,
Borrows its saddest tongue from jest,
Thou hast of absence so create
A presence more importunate;
And thy voice pleads its sweetest suit
When it is mute.
I thank the once accursed star
Which did me teach
To make of Silence my familiar,
Who hath the rich reversion of thy speech,
Since the most charming sounds thy thought can wear,
Cast off, fall to that pale attendant's share;
And thank the gift which made my mind
A shadow-world, wherethrough the shadows wind
Of all the loved and lovely of my kind.

Like a maiden Saxon, folden,
As she flits, in moon-drenched mist;
Whose curls streaming flaxen-golden,
By the misted moonbeams kist,
Dispread their filmy floating silk
Like honey steeped in milk:
So, vague goldenness remote,
Through my thoughts I watch thee float.
When the snake summer casts her blazoned skin
We find it at the turn of autumn's path,
And think it summer that rewinded hath,
Joying therein;
And this enamouring slough of thee, mine elf,
I take it for thyself;
Content. Content? Yea, title it content.
The very loves that belt thee must prevent
My love, I know, with their legitimacy:
As the metallic vapours, that are swept
Athwart the sun, in his light intercept
The very hues
Which THEIR conflagrant elements effuse.
But, my love, my heart, my fair,
That only I should see thee rare,
Or tent to the hid core thy rarity,
This were a mournfulness more piercing far
Than that those other loves my own must bar,
Or thine for others leave thee none for me.

But on a day whereof I think,

One shall dip his hand to drink
In that still water of thy soul,
And its imaged tremors race
Over thy joy-troubled face,
As the intervolved reflections roll
From a shaken fountain's brink,
With swift light wrinkling its alcove.
From the hovering wing of Love
The warm stain shall flit roseal on thy cheek,
Then, sweet blushet! whenas he,
The destined paramount of thy universe,
Who has no worlds to sigh for, ruling thee,
Ascends his vermeil throne of empery,
One grace alone I seek.
Oh! may this treasure-galleon of my verse,
Fraught with its golden passion, oared with cadent rhyme,
Set with a towering press of fantasies,
Drop safely down the time,
Leaving mine isled self behind it far
Soon to be sunken in the abysm of seas,
(As down the years the splendour voyages
From some long ruined and night-submerged star),
And in thy subject sovereign's havening heart
Anchor the freightage of its virgin ore;
Adding its wasteful more
To his own overflowing treasury.
So through his river mine shall reach thy sea,
Bearing its confluent part;
In his pulse mine shall thrill;
And the quick heart shall quicken from the heart that's still.

Ah! help, my Daemon that hast served me well!
Not at this last, oh, do not me disgrace!
I faint, I sicken, darkens all my sight,
As, poised upon this unprevisioned height,
I lift into its place
The utmost aery traceried pinnacle.
So; it is builded, the high tenement,
- God grant to mine intent!
Most like a palace of the Occident,
Up-thrusting, toppling maze on maze,
Its mounded blaze,
And washed by the sunset's rosy waves,
Whose sea drinks rarer hue from those rare walls it laves.
Yet wail, my spirits, wail!
So few therein to enter shall prevail!
Scarce fewer could win way, if their desire
A dragon baulked, with involuted spire,
And writhen snout spattered with yeasty fire.
For at the elfin portal hangs a horn
Which none can wind aright

Save the appointed knight
Whose lids the fay-wings brushed when he was born.
All others stray forlorn,
Or glimpsing, through the blazoned windows scrolled
Receding labyrinths lessening tortuously
In half obscurity;
With mystic images, inhuman, cold,
That flameless torches hold.
But who can wind that horn of might
(The horn of dead Heliades) aright,
Straight
Open for him shall roll the conscious gate;
And light leap up from all the torches there,
And life leap up in every torchbearer,
And the stone faces kindle in the glow,
And into the blank eyes the irids grow,
And through the dawning irids ambushed meanings show.
Illumined this wise on,
He threads securely the far intricacies,
With brede from Heaven's wrought vesture overstrewn;
Swift Tellus' purfled tunic, girt upon
With the blown chlamys of her fluttering seas;
And the freaked kirtle of the pearled moon:
Until he gain the structure's core, where stands -
A toil of magic hands -
The unbodied spirit of the sorcerer,
Most strangely rare,
As is a vision remembered in the noon;
Unbodied, yet to mortal seeing clear,
Like sighs exhaled in eager atmosphere.
From human haps and mutabilities
It rests exempt, beneath the edifice
To which itself gave rise;
Sustaining centre to the bubble of stone
Which, breathed from it, exists by it alone.
Yea, ere Saturnian earth her child consumes,
And I lie down with outworn ossuaries,
Ere death's grim tongue anticipates the tomb's
Siste viator, in this storied urn
My living heart is laid to throb and burn,
Till end be ended, and till ceasing cease.

And thou by whom this strain hath parentage;
Wantoner between the yet untreacherous claws
Of newly-whelped existence! ere he pause,
What gift to thee can yield the archimage?
For coming seasons' frets
What aids, what amulets,
What softenings, or what brightenings?
As Thunder writhes the lash of his long lightnings
About the growling heads of the brute main

Foaming at mouth, until it wallow again
In the scooped oozes of its bed of pain;
So all the gnashing jaws, the leaping heads
Of hungry menaces, and of ravening dreads,
Of pangs
Twitch-lipped, with quivering nostrils and immitigate fangs,
I scourge beneath the torment of my charms
That their repentless nature fear to work thee harms.
And as yon Apollonian harp-player,
Yon wandering psalterist of the sky,
With flickering strings which scatter melody,
The silver-stoled damsels of the sea,
Or lake, or fount, or stream,
Enchants from their ancestral heaven of waters
To Naiad it through the unfrothing air;
My song enchants so out of undulous dream
The glimmering shapes of its dim-tressed daughters,
And missions each to be thy minister.
Saying; 'O ye,
The organ-stops of being's harmony;
The blushes on existence's pale face,
Lending it sudden grace;
Without whom we should but guess Heaven's worth
By blank negations of this sordid earth,
(So haply to the blind may light
Be but gloom's undetermined opposite);
Ye who are thus as the refracting air
Whereby we see Heaven's sun before it rise
Above the dull line of our mortal skies;
As breathing on the strained ear that sighs
From comrades viewless unto strained eyes,
Soothing our terrors in the lampless night;
Ye who can make this world where all is deeming
What world ye list, being arbiters of seeming;
Attend upon her ways, benignant powers!
Unroll ye life a carpet for her feet,
And cast ye down before them blossomy hours,
Until her going shall be clogged with sweet!
All dear emotions whose new-bathed hair,
Still streaming from the soul, in love's warm air
Smokes with a mist of tender fantasies;
All these,
And all the heart's wild growths which, swiftly bright,
Spring up the crimson agarics of a night,
No pain in withering, yet a joy arisen;
And all thin shapes more exquisitely rare,
More subtly fair,
Than these weak ministering words have spell to prison
Within the magic circle of this rhyme;
And all the fays who in our creedless clime
Have sadly ceased

Bearing to other children childhood's proper feast;
Whose robes are fluent crystal, crocus-hued,
Whose wings are wind a-fire, whose mantles wrought
From spray that falling rainbows shake
These, ye familiars to my wizard thought,
Make things of journal custom unto her;
With lucent feet imbrued,
If young Day tread, a glorious vintager,
The wine-press of the purple-foamed east;
Or round the nodding sun, flush-faced and sunken,
His wild bacchantes drunken
Reel, with rent woofs a-flaunt, their westering rout.
- But lo! at length the day is lingered out,
At length my Ariel lays his viol by;
We sing no more to thee, child, he and I;
The day is lingered out:
In slow wreaths folden
Around yon censer, sphered, golden,
Vague Vesper's fumes aspire;
And glimmering to eclipse
The long laburnum drips
Its honey of wild flame, its jocund spilth of fire.

Now pass your ways, fair bird, and pass your ways,
If you will;
I have you through the days!
A flit or hold you still,
And perch you where you list
On what wrist,
You are mine through the times!
I have caught you fast for ever in a tangle of sweet rhymes.
And in your young maiden morn,
You may scorn,
But you must be
Bound and sociate to me;
With this thread from out the tomb my dead hand shall tether thee!

Go, sister-songs, to that sweet sister-pair
For whom I have your frail limbs fashioned,
And framed feateously;
For whom I have your frail limbs fashioned
With how great shamefastness and how great dread,
Knowing you frail, but not if you be fair,
Though framed feateously;
Go unto them from me.
Go from my shadow to their sunshine sight,
Made for all sights' delight;
Go like twin swans that oar the surgy storms
To bate with pennoned snows in candent air:
Nigh with abased head,
Yourselves linked sisterly, that sister-pair,

And go in presence there;
Saying 'Your young eyes cannot see our forms,
Nor read the yearning of our looks aright;
But time shall trail the veilings from our hair,
And cleanse your seeing with his euphrasy,
(Yea, even your bright seeing make more bright,
Which is all sights' delight),
And ye shall know us for what things we be.

'Whilom, within a poet's calyxed heart,
A dewy love we trembled all apart;
Whence it took rise
Beneath your radiant eyes,
Which misted it to music. We must long,
A floating haze of silver subtile song,
Await love-laden
Above each maiden
The appointed hour that o'er the hearts of you
As vapours into dew
Unweave, whence they were wove,
Shall turn our loosening musics back to love.'

Memorat Memoria

Come you living or dead to me, out of the silt of the Past,
With the sweet of the piteous first, and the shame of the shameful last?
Come with your dear and dreadful face through the passes of Sleep,
The terrible mask, and the face it masked the face you did not keep?
You are neither two nor one I would you were one or two,
For your awful self is embalmed in the fragrant self I knew:
And Above may ken, and Beneath may ken, what I mean by these words of whirl,
But by my sleep that sleepeth not, O Shadow of a Girl!
Nought here but I and my dreams shall know the secret of this thing:
For ever the songs I sing are sad with the songs I never sing,
Sad are sung songs, but how more sad the songs we dare not sing!

Ah, the ill that we do in tenderness, and the hateful horror of love!
It has sent more souls to the unslaked Pit than it ever will draw above.
I damned you, girl, with my pity, who had better by far been thwart,
And drave you hard on the track to hell, because I was gentle of heart.
I shall have no comfort now in scent, no ease in dew, for this;
I shall be afraid of daffodils, and rose-buds are amiss;
You have made a thing of innocence as shameful as a sin,
I shall never feel a girl's soft arms without horror of the skin.
My child! what was it that I sowed, that I so ill should reap?
You have done this to me. And I, what I to you? It lies with Sleep.

Epilogue - To The Poet's Sitter

Wherein he excuseth himself for the manner of the Portrait.

Alas! now wilt thou chide, and say (I deem),
My figured descant hides the simple theme:
Or in another wise reproving, say
I ill observe thine own high reticent way.
Oh, pardon, that I testify of thee
What thou couldst never speak, nor others be!

Yet (for the book is not more innocent
Of what the gazer's eyes makes so intent),
She will but smile, perhaps, that I find my fair
Sufficing scope in such strait theme as her.
'Bird of the sun! the stars' wild honey-bee!
Is your gold browsing done so thoroughly?
Or sinks a singed wing to narrow nest in me?'
(Thus she might say: for not this lowly vein
Out-deprecates her deprecating strain.)
Oh, you mistake, dear lady, quite; nor know
Ether was strict as you, its loftiness as low!

The heavens do not advance their majesty
Over their marge; beyond his empery
The ensigns of the wind are not unfurled,
His reign is hooped in by the pale o' the world.
'Tis not the continent, but the contained,
That pleasaunce makes or prison, loose or chained.
Too much alike or little captives me,
For all oppression is captivity.
What groweth to its height demands no higher;
The limit limits not, but the desire.
Give but my spirit its desired scope,
A giant in a pismire, I not grope;
Deny it, and an ant, with on my back
A firmament, the skiey vault will crack.
Our minds make their own Termini, nor call
The issuing circumscriptions great or small;
So high constructing Nature lessons to us all:
Who optics gives accommodate to see
Your countenance large as looks the sun to be,
And distant greatness less than near humanity.

We, therefore, with a sure instinctive mind,
An equal spaciousness of bondage find
In confines far or near, of air or our own kind.
Our looks and longings, which affront the stars,
Most richly bruised against their golden bars,
Delighted captives of their flaming spears,
Find a restraint restrainless which appears
As that is, and so simply natural,
In you; the fair detention freedom call,
And overscroll with fancies the loved prison-wall.

Such sweet captivity, and only such,
In you, as in those golden bars, we touch!
Our gazes for sufficing limits know
The firmament above, your face below;
Our longings are contented with the skies,
Contented with the heaven, and your eyes.
My restless wings, that beat the whole world through,
Flag on the confines of the sun and you;
And find the human pale remoter of the two.

Her Portrait

Oh, but the heavenly grammar did I hold
Of that high speech which angels' tongues turn gold!
So should her deathless beauty take no wrong,
Praised in her own great kindred's fit and cognate tongue.
Or if that language yet with us abode.
Which Adam in the garden talked with God!
But our untempered speech descends poor heirs!
Grimy and rough-cast still from Babel's bricklayers:
Curse on the brutish jargon we inherit,
Strong but to damn, not memorise, a spirit!
A cheek, a lip, a limb, a bosom, they
Move with light ease in speech of working-day;
And women we do use to praise even so.
But here the gates we burst, and to the temple go.
Their praise were her dispraise; who dare, who dare,
Adulate the seraphim for their burning hair?
How, if with them I dared, here should I dare it?
How praise the woman, who but know the spirit?
How praise the colour of her eyes, uncaught
While they were coloured with her varying thought
How her mouth's shape, who only use to know
What tender shape her speech will fit it to?
Or her lips' redness, when their joined veil
Song's fervid hand has parted till it wore them pale?

If I would praise her soul (temerarious if!),
All must be mystery and hieroglyph.
Heaven, which not oft is prodigal of its more
To singers, in their song too great before;
By which the hierarch of large poesy is
Restrained to his once sacred benefice;
Only for her the salutary awe
Relaxes and stern canon of its law;
To her alone concedes pluralities,
In her alone to reconcile agrees
The Muse, the Graces, and the Charities;
To her, who can the trust so well conduct
To her it gives the use, to us the usufruct.

What of the dear administress then may
I utter, though I spoke her own carved perfect way?
What of her daily gracious converse known,
Whose heavenly despotism must needs dethrone
And subjugate all sweetness but its own?
Deep in my heart subsides the infrequent word,
And there dies slowly throbbing like a wounded bird.
What of her silence, that outsweetens speech?
What of her thoughts, high marks for mine own thoughts to reach?
Yet (Chaucer's antique sentence so to turn),
Most gladly will she teach, and gladly learn;
And teaching her, by her enchanting art,
The master threefold learns for all he can impart.
Now all is said, and all being said, aye me!
There yet remains unsaid the very She.
Nay, to conclude (so to conclude I dare),
If of her virtues you evade the snare,
Then for her faults you'll fall in love with her.

Alas, and I have spoken of her Muse -
Her Muse, that died with her auroral dews!
Learn, the wise cherubim from harps of gold
Seduce a trepidating music manifold;
But the superior seraphim do know
None other music but to flame and glow.
So she first lighted on our frosty earth,
A sad musician, of cherubic birth,
Playing to alien ears which did not prize
The uncomprehended music of the skies
The exiled airs of her far Paradise.
But soon from her own harpings taking fire,
In love and light her melodies expire.
Now Heaven affords her, for her silenced hymn,
A double portion of the seraphim.

At the rich odours from her heart that rise,
My soul remembers its lost Paradise,
And antenatal gales blow from Heaven's shores of spice;
I grow essential all, uncloaking me
From this encumbering virility,
And feel the primal sex of heaven and poetry:
And parting from her, in me linger on
Vague snatches of Uranian antiphon.

How to the petty prison could she shrink
Of femineity? Nay, but I think
In a dear courtesy her spirit would
Woman assume, for grace to womanhood.
Or, votaress to the virgin Sanctitude
Of reticent withdrawal's sweet, courted pale,
She took the cloistral flesh, the sexual veil,

Of her sad, aboriginal sisterhood;
The habit of cloistral flesh which founding Eve indued.

Thus do I know her: but for what men call
Beauty the loveliness corporeal,
Its most just praise a thing unproper were
To singer or to listener, me or her.
She wears that body but as one indues
A robe, half careless, for it is the use;
Although her soul and it so fair agree,
We sure may, unattaint of heresy,
Conceit it might the soul's begetter be.
The immortal could we cease to contemplate,
The mortal part suggests its every trait.
God laid His fingers on the ivories
Of her pure members as on smoothed keys,
And there out-breathed her spirit's harmonies
I'll speak a little proudly:- I disdain
To count the beauty worth my wish or gaze,
Which the dull daily fool can covet or obtain.
I do confess the fairness of the spoil,
But from such rivalry it takes a soil.
For her I'll proudlier speak:- how could it be
That I should praise the gilding on the psaltery?
'Tis not for her to hold that prize a prize,
Or praise much praise, though proudest in its wise,
To which even hopes of merely women rise.
Such strife would to the vanquished laurels yield,
Against HER suffered to have lost a field.
Herself must with herself be sole compeer,
Unless the people of her distant sphere
Some gold migration send to melodise the year.
But first our hearts must burn in larger guise,
To reformate the uncharitable skies,
And so the deathless plumage to acclimatise:
Since this, their sole congener in our clime,
Droops her sad, ruffled thoughts for half the shivering time.

Yet I have felt what terrors may consort
In women's cheeks, the Graces' soft resort;
My hand hath shook at gentle hands' access,
And trembled at the waving of a tress;
My blood known panic fear, and fled dismayed,
Where ladies' eyes have set their ambuscade.
The rustle of a robe hath been to me
The very rattle of love's musketry;
Although my heart hath beat the loud advance,
I have recoiled before a challenging glance,
Proved gay alarms where warlike ribbons dance.
And from it all, this knowledge have I got, -
The whole that others have, is less than they have not;

All which makes other women noted fair,
Unnoted would remain and overshone in her.

How should I gauge what beauty is her dole,
Who cannot see her countenance for her soul;
As birds see not the casement for the sky?
And as 'tis check they prove its presence by,
I know not of her body till I find
My flight debarred the heaven of her mind.
Hers is the face whence all should copied be,
Did God make replicas of such as she;
Its presence felt by what it does abate,
Because the soul shines through tempered and mitigate:
Where as a figure labouring at night
Beside the body of a splendid light
Dark Time works hidden by its luminousness;
And every line he labours to impress
Turns added beauty, like the veins that run
Athwart a leaf which hangs against the sun.

There regent Melancholy wide controls;
There Earth- and Heaven-Love play for aureoles;
There Sweetness out of Sadness breaks at fits,
Like bubbles on dark water, or as flits
A sudden silver fin through its deep infinites;
There amorous Thought has sucked pale Fancy's breath,
And Tenderness sits looking toward the lands of death
There Feeling stills her breathing with her hand,
And Dream from Melancholy part wrests the wand
And on this lady's heart, looked you so deep,
Poor Poetry has rocked himself to sleep:
Upon the heavy blossom of her lips
Hangs the bee Musing; nigh her lids eclipse
Each half-occulted star beneath that lies;
And in the contemplation of those eyes,
Passionless passion, wild tranquillities.

The Poppy

To Monica

Summer set lip to earth's bosom bare,
And left the flushed print in a poppy there:
Like a yawn of fire from the grass it came,
And the fanning wind puffed it to flapping flame.

With burnt mouth, red like a lion's, it drank
The blood of the sun as he slaughtered sank,
And dipped its cup in the purpurate shine
When the Eastern conduits ran with wine.

Till it grew lethargied with fierce bliss,
And hot as a swinked gipsy is,
And drowsed in sleepy savageries,
With mouth wide a-pout for a sultry kiss.

A child and man paced side by side,
Treading the skirts of eventide;
But between the clasp of his hand and hers
Lay, felt not, twenty withered years.

She turned, with the rout of her dusk South hair,
And saw the sleeping gipsy there:
And snatched and snapped it in swift child's whim,
With "Keep it, long as you live!" to him.

And his smile, as nymphs from their laving meres,
Trembled up from a bath of tears;
And joy, like a mew sea-rocked apart,
Tossed on the wave of his troubled heart.

For he saw what she did not see,
That as kindled by its own fervency
The verge shrivelled inward smoulderingly:
And suddenly 'twixt his hand and hers
He knew the twenty withered years
No flower, but twenty shrivelled years.

"Was never such thing until this hour,"
Low to his heart he said; "the flower
Of sleep brings wakening to me,
And of oblivion, memory."

"Was never this thing to me," he said,
"Though with bruisèd poppies my feet are red!"
And again to his own heart very low:
"O child! I love, for I love and know;

"But you, who love nor know at all
The diverse chambers in Love's guest-hall,
Where some rise early, few sit long:
In how differing accents hear the throng
His great Pentecostal tongue;

"Who know not love from amity,
Nor my reported self from me;
A fair fit gift is this, meseems,
You give this withering flower of dreams.

"O frankly fickle, and fickly true,
Do you know what the days will do to you?
To your love and you what the days will do,

O frankly fickle, and fickly true?

"You have loved me, Fair, three lives or days:
'Twill pass with the passing of my face.
But where I go, your face goes too,
To watch lest I play false to you.

"I am but, my sweet, your foster-lover,
Knowing well when certain years are over
You vanish from me to another;
Yet I know, and love, like the foster-mother.

"So, frankly fickle, and fickly true!
For my brief life while I take from you
This token, fair and fit, meseems,
For me this withering flower of dreams."

The sleep-flower sways in the wheat its head,
Heavy with dreams, as that with bread:
The goodly grain and the sun-flushed sleeper
The reaper reaps, and Time the reaper.

I hang 'mid men my needless head,
And my fruit is dreams, as theirs is bread:
The goodly men and the sun-hazed sleeper
Time shall reap, but after the reaper
The world shall glean of me, me the sleeper.

Love, love! your flower of withered dream
In leavèd rhyme lies safe, I deem,
Sheltered and shut in a nook of rhyme,
From the reaper man, and his reaper Time.

Love! I fall into the claws of Time:
But lasts within a leavèd rhyme
All that the world of me esteems
My withered dreams, my withered dreams.

A Judgment In Heaven

Athwart the sod which is treading for God the poet paced with his splendid eyes;
Paradise-verdure he stately passes to win to the Father of Paradise,
Through the conscious and palpitant grasses of inter-tangled relucent dyes.

The angels a-play on its fields of Summer (their wild wings rustled his guides' cymars)
Looked up from disport at the passing comer, as they pelted each other with handfuls of stars;
And the warden-spirits with startled feet rose, hand on sword, by their tethered cars.

With plumes night-tinctured englobed and cinctured, of Saints, his guided steps held on
To where on the far crystelline pale of that transtellar Heaven there shone
The immutable crocean dawn effusing from the Father's Throne.

Through the reverberant Eden-ways the bruit of his great advent driven,
Back from the fulgent justle and press with mighty echoing so was given,
As when the surly thunder smites upon the clanged gates of Heaven.

Over the bickering gonfalons, far-ranged as for Tartarean wars,
Went a waver of ribbed fire as night-seas on phosphoric bars
Like a flame-plumed fan shake slowly out their ridgy reach of crumbling stars.

At length to where on His fretted Throne sat in the heart of His aged dominions
The great Triune, and Mary nigh, lit round with spears of their hauberked minions,
The poet drew, in the thunderous blue involved dread of those mounted pinions.

As in a secret and tenebrous cloud the watcher from the disquiet earth
At momentary intervals beholds from its ragged rifts break forth
The flash of a golden perturbation, the travelling threat of a witched birth;

Till heavily parts a sinister chasm, a grisly jaw, whose verges soon,
Slowly and ominously filled by the on-coming plenilune,
Supportlessly congest with fire, and suddenly spit forth the moon:

With beauty, not terror, through tangled error of night-dipt plumes so burned their charge;
Swayed and parted the globing clusters so, disclosed from their kindling marge,
Roseal-chapleted, splendent-vestured, the singer there where God's light lay large.

Hu, hu! a wonder! a wonder! see, clasping the singer's glories clings
A dingy creature, even to laughter cloaked and clad in patchwork things,
Shrinking close from the unused glows of the seraphs' versicoloured wings.

A rhymer, rhyming a futile rhyme, he had crept for convoy through Eden-ways
Into the shade of the poet's glory, darkened under his prevalent rays,
Fearfully hoping a distant welcome as a poor kinsman of his lays.

The angels laughed with a lovely scorning: 'Who has done this sorry deed in
The garden of our Father, God? 'mid his blossoms to sow this weed in?
Never our fingers knew this stuff: not so fashion the looms of Eden!'

The singer bowed his brow majestic, searching that patchwork through and through,
Feeling God's lucent gazes traverse his singing-stoling and spirit too:
The hallowed harpers were fain to frown on the strange thing come 'mid their sacred crew,
Only the singer that was earth his fellow-earth and his own self knew.

But the poet rent off robe and wreath, so as a sloughing serpent doth,
Laid them at the rhymer's feet, shed down wreath and raiment both,
Stood in a dim and shamed stole, like the tattered wing of a musty moth.

'Thou gav'st the weed and wreath of song, the weed and wreath are solely Thine,
And this dishonest vesture is the only vesture that is mine;
The life I textured, Thou the song MY handicraft is not divine!'

He wrested o'er the rhymer's head that garmenting which wrought him wrong;

A flickering tissue argentine down dripped its shivering silvers long:
'Better thou wov'st thy woof of life than thou didst weave thy woof of song!'

Never a chief in Saintdom was, but turned him from the Poet then;
Never an eye looked mild on him 'mid all the angel myriads ten,
Save sinless Mary, and sinful Mary the Mary titled Magdalen.

'Turn yon robe,' spake Magdalen, 'of torn bright song, and see and feel.'
They turned the raiment, saw and felt what their turning did reveal
All the inner surface piled with bloodied hairs, like hairs of steel.

'Take, I pray, yon chaplet up, thrown down ruddied from his head.'
They took the roseal chaplet up, and they stood astonished:
Every leaf between their fingers, as they bruised it, burst and bled.

'See his torn flesh through those rents; see the punctures round his hair,
As if the chaplet-flowers had driven deep roots in to nourish there
Lord, who gav'st him robe and wreath, WHAT was this Thou gav'st for wear?'

'Fetch forth the Paradisal garb!' spake the Father, sweet and low;
Drew them both by the frightened hand where Mary's throne made irised bow
'Take, Princess Mary, of thy good grace, two spirits greater than they know.'

"Manus Animam Pinxit"

Lady who hold'st on me dominion!
Within your spirit's arms I stay me fast
Against the fell
Immitigate ravening of the gates of hell;
And claim my right in you, most hardly won,
Of chaste fidelity upon the chaste:
Hold me and hold by me, lest both should fall
(O in high escalade high companion!)
Even in the breach of Heaven's assaulted wall.
Like to a wind-sown sapling grow I from
The clift, Sweet, of your skyward-jetting soul,
Shook by all gusts that sweep it, overcome
By all its clouds incumbent: O be true
To your soul, dearest, as my life to you!
For if that soil grow sterile, then the whole
Of me must shrivel, from the topmost shoot
Of climbing poesy, and my life, killed through,
Dry down and perish to the foodless root.

Sweet Summer! unto you this swallow drew,
By secret instincts inappeasable,
That did direct him well,
Lured from his gelid North which wrought him wrong,
Wintered of sunning song;
By happy instincts inappeasable,
Ah yes! that led him well,

Lured to the untried regions and the new
Climes of auspicious you;
To twitter there, and in his singing dwell.
But ah! if you, my Summer, should grow waste,
With grieving skies o'ercast,
For such migration my poor wing was strong
But once; it has no power to fare again
Forth o'er the heads of men,
Nor other Summers for its Sanctuary:
But from your mind's chilled sky
It needs must drop, and lie with stiffened wings
Among your soul's forlornest things;
A speck upon your memory, alack!
A dead fly in a dusty window-crack.

O therefore you who are
What words, being to such mysteries
As raiment to the body is,
Should rather hide than tell;
Chaste and intelligential love:
Whose form is as a grove
Hushed with the cooing of an unseen dove;
Whose spirit to my touch thrills purer far
Than is the tingling of a silver bell;
Whose body other ladies well might bear
As soul, yea, which it profanation were
For all but you to take as fleshly woof,
Being spirit truest proof;
Whose spirit sure is lineal to that
Which sang Magnificat:
Chastest, since such you are,
Take this curbed spirit of mine,
Which your own eyes invest with light divine,
For lofty love and high auxiliar
In daily exalt emprise
Which outsoars mortal eyes;
This soul which on your soul is laid,
As maid's breast against breast of maid;
Beholding how your own I have engraved
On it, and with what purging thoughts have laved
This love of mine from all mortality
Indeed the copy is a painful one,
And with long labour done!
O if you doubt the thing you are, lady,
Come then, and look in me;
Your beauty, Dian, dress and contemplate
Within a pool to Dian consecrate!
Unveil this spirit, lady, when you will,
For unto all but you 'tis veiled still:
Unveil, and fearless gaze there, you alone,
And if you love the image - 'tis your own!

Scala Jacobi Portaque Eburnea

Her soul from earth to Heaven lies,
Like the ladder of the vision,
Whereon go
To and fro,
In ascension and demission,
Star-flecked feet of Paradise.

Now she is drawn up from me,
All my angels, wet-eyed, tristful,
Gaze from great
Heaven's gate
Like pent children, very wistful,
That below a playmate see.

Dream-dispensing face of hers!
Ivory port which loosed upon me
Wings, I wist,
Whose amethyst
Trepidations have forgone me,
Hesper's filmy traffickers!

Gilded Gold

Thou dost to rich attire a grace,
To let it deck itself with thee,
And teachest pomp strange cunning ways
To be thought simplicity.
But lilies, stolen from grassy mold,
No more curled state unfold
Translated to a vase of gold;
In burning throne though they keep still
Serenities unthawed and chill.
Therefore, albeit thou'rt stately so,
In statelier state thou us'dst to go.

Though jewels should phosphoric burn
Through those night-waters of thine hair,
A flower from its translucid urn
Poured silver flame more lunar-fair.
These futile trappings but recall
Degenerate worshippers who fall
In purfled kirtle and brocade
To 'parel the white Mother-Maid.
For, as her image stood arrayed
In vests of its self-substance wrought

To measure of the sculptor's thought
Slurred by those added braveries;

So for thy spirit did devise
Its Maker seemly garniture,
Of its own essence parcel pure,
From grave simplicities a dress,
And reticent demurenesses,
And love encinctured with reserve;
Which the woven vesture should subserve.
For outward robes in their ostents
Should show the soul's habiliments.
Therefore I say,--Thou'rt fair even so,
But better Fair I use to know.

The violet would thy dusk hair deck
With graces like thine own unsought.
Ah! but such place would daze and wreck
Its simple, lowly rustic thought.
For so advanced, dear, to thee,
It would unlearn humility!
Yet do not, with an altered look,
In these weak numbers read rebuke;
Which are but jealous lest too much
God's master-piece thou shouldst retouch.
Where a sweetness is complete,
Add not sweets unto the sweet!
Or, as thou wilt, for others so
In unfamiliar richness go;
But keep for mine acquainted eyes
The fashions of thy Paradise.

Dream Tryst

The breaths of kissing night and day
Were mingled in the eastern Heaven:
Throbbing with unheard melody
Shook Lyra all its star-chord seven:
When dusk shrunk cold, and light trod shy,
And dawn's grey eyes were troubled grey;
And souls went palely up the sky,
And mine to Lucide.

There was no change in her sweet eyes
Since last I saw those sweet eyes shine;
There was no change in her deep heart
Since last that deep heart knocked at mine.
Her eyes were clear, her eyes were Hope's,
Wherein did ever come and go
The sparkle of the fountain-drops
From her sweet soul below.

The chambers in the house of dreams
Are fed with so divine an air,

That Time's hoar wings grow young therein,
And they who walk there are most fair.
I joyed for me, I joyed for her,
Who with the Past meet girt about:
Where our last kiss still warms the air,
Nor can her eyes go out.

www.ingramcontent.com/pod-product-compliance
Lightning Source LLC
LaVergne TN
LVHW010545100826
845148LV00013B/2616

* 9 7 8 1 7 8 3 9 4 9 3 3 5 *